How to Create Value First and Other Lessons

Helping Organizations Go from Surviving to Thriving

Bryan M. Balch

Published by Bryan M. Balch
at CreateSpace

Copyright October 2014
Bryan M. Balch

ISBN-13: 978-1502742230
ISBN-10: 1502742233
CreateSpace Title ID: 4904532
License Notes

This publication is available in paperback and ebook formats. It will soon be available as an audiobook.

The ebook publication of this book is licensed for your personal enjoyment only. This ebook may not be re-sold or given away to other people. If you would like to share this book with another person, please purchase an additional copy for each recipient. If you're reading this book and did not purchase it, or it was not purchased for your use only, then please return to Amazon.com and purchase your own copy. Thank you for respecting the hard work of this author.

Table of Contents

Dedication 6
Acknowledgments 8
Introduction 9
Explaining Indirect Benefits Expands Support 11
Only Ask Others To Do, What You Do 15
Use Problems To Create Opportunities 20
Connected Donors Become Partners 25
By Offering More Value, You Increase Revenues 29
It's Amazing What You Can Accomplish If You Don't Care Who Gets The Credit 33
If You Want Others To Contribute, Contribute To Others 37
Do The Work And The Money Will Come 41
If Meetings Are A Must, Bring A Must To The Meetings 46
Solving A Problem Generates More Funds Than Complaining 52
Use Creativity To Grow Your Funds 58
You Can't Be Too Big To Do The Little Things 64
Your Network Equals Your Net Worth 70
If You're Not Helping Row The Boat, You're An Anchor 78
Do You Know What An Outhouse Is 85
Sometimes Two Organizations Are Better Than One 94
About The Author 97
To Connect With Bryan 100
Consultations And Presentations 100
Other Publications 100
Added Bonus(es) 101

Third Bonus 101

Dedication

This book is dedicated to everyone I have interacted with in my career.

When I say everyone, I mean everyone. Owners, board members, supervisors, employees, volunteers, clients, representatives from contracting agencies, collaborative agencies' employees, coaches, mentors and countless others.

Regardless of whether our paths crossed just long enough to say hello or we spent enough time together to taste the sweetness and the bitterness that comes with the highs and lows of working with people.

I am thankful for each and every one of you. You all have played a role in helping me get to where I am today.

Believe it or not, it's the individuals that cause us the most frustration, the betrayals, the ones that test our faith in others, that cause us to question our own path in life, that in the long run, benefit us the most.

It's truly when we overcome obstacles, rebuild our trust in others, and learn how to solve problems, that we grow into better people, better leaders, better mentors.

I include the employees that took guidance, that gave me the opportunity to watch them grow and become more than they were when we met.

I include the clients that were able to use the services we offered to become more independent, to improve their situation, their family life, and so much more. Each success story added to our belief that what we were doing mattered and made a difference.

I include the relationships that were built, many of which are stronger today than ever before, within the organizations and with the funders, the collaborations, and the communities.

When you get right down to it, all business is relationships. Life is relationships. The quality of your business, the quality of your life will equal the quality of your relationships.

I am grateful and blessed for all of my relationships.

Acknowledgments

I truly want to acknowledge the individuals and groups that have hired me and partnered with me throughout my career.

Whether you were a Supervisor, the HR Department, an individual owner, part of a hiring committee, or a board of directors, you all share one thing in common.

I also want to include current and future partnerships as well. You may be a new client seeking individual improvement or an organization seeking guidance, or new affiliate partners wanting to improve their financial future, you also share one thing in common.

Past, present and future, the one thing you have in common, is you each had (and have) enough faith and belief in me to give me a chance.

While all of my employment has some similarities, each position offered something new for me. Each new position, each consultation, each new business partner, has brought new challenges, something I had no previous experience doing.

I've been blessed to be put in uncomfortable positions, requiring me to learn, grow and stretch.

I want to acknowledge and thank my parents for instilling confidence in me. Every opportunity has been like stepping into the unknown. It is because of them, I've always been confident I would succeed.

I acknowledge and thank all of you from the bottom of my heart. I believe we've grown through our accomplishments, periods of opposition, differences of opinion, and times of celebration.

Introduction

The sole purpose of this book is to help leaders and their respective organizations grow and prosper. This book provides examples and action steps to help others along the way to do the same.

The lessons I've learned and share in this book are based on actual experiences over the past 25 years, while leading various organizations and as a consultant, coach and trainer to other organizations.

While the book is written primarily for the non-profit sector, the principles can be applied to large and small businesses, as well as sole proprietors.

It is my hope this book will help individuals and organizations, regardless of their current situation, to view the future more optimistically, to give new perspective, share ideas and spark new ideas.

I believe everyone that reads this book, will discover at least one golden nugget, one idea, that will create a new partnership, a new funding stream, and/or better ways to publicize the impact their respective organizations have in the communities they serve.

I suggest every board member, executive director, and management team read this book. This will help create new perspective, better understanding, more support, and help to establish a stronger, clearer vision for leaders and organizations.

My hope for you and your organization is that you celebrate small successes as they will accumulate into long term success; that you experience enough opposition and obstacles to keep you learning and growing; and that your legacy will be you impacted the lives of many.

I want to congratulate you on the purchase of this book! Leaders are readers. Leaders are continually working on self-improvement. As you learn and grow, you are able to continue helping others to do the same.

If you received a copy of this book as a gift, you should feel good knowing someone is interested in your development, your growth, and your success.

There is greatness with you. There is potential in all of us. It is our individual commitment to personal growth that will determine how much of our potential is fulfilled.

In closing, I wish you continuing success in your life's journey. The purpose of life is service to others. I pray this book will be of service to you.

With my respect, appreciation, and gratitude,

Your partner in success,

Bryan M. Balch

Lesson # 1

Explaining Indirect Benefits Expands Support

I believe it takes all of the community services and community based organizations to make a community whole. Each organization serves a population. If that organization goes under, those people that were being served are going to suffer. They will either go without services or they will have to go to another organization that is now trying to pick up the slack from the now-defunct organization. This translates into diminished services, because the organization taking on the new services are trying to do more with less.

I share these thoughts as they were going through my mind as I walked to the podium to address a City Council on why our organization deserved funding.

While sitting in the audience, awaiting my turn to speak, I listened as the Fire Chief laid out the needs for additional funding to keep their fire houses open. He was followed by a spokesperson for the Police Department pointing out their needs for additional funding to increase their staff to fight increasing crime. The Executive Director of Meals on Wheels needed additional funding to keep up with rising costs and an increasing number of seniors. The last one to speak before me was a representative for a local assisted housing program requesting additional funds to offset rising medical costs.

I began by sharing my beliefs as written above. I pointed out each of the mentioned organizational needs are legitimate. There will be negative effects if those needs aren't met.

The needs of those organizations will continue to grow.

While legitimate, they are also like a black hole. No matter how good they are, there will be growing needs as the community grows and grows older.

I was representing an organization that was asking for $3,000. Our organization's mission was to help individuals with disabilities to live as independently as possible. For some, this meant home modifications to allow wheelchair access after a stroke or accident. For others it was advocating for disability benefits because they could no longer work. For some it was re-training so they could re-enter the workplace.

I asked the City Council, if they couldn't award our organization the full $3,000, to consider a smaller amount. I explained even $1,000 would help. Receiving funds from the City would allow me to leverage them for federal funds.

I pointed out that when applying for funds from Washington, D.C., they have no idea how good an organization located clear across the country is. In almost all federal grant applications, they ask "who are your current funders." They are looking for "stamps of approval." Their argument (and it's a good one) is if your own city won't fund you, why should we?

I laid out my plans to apply for federal grants in excess of $100,000 that would serve the city residents. Any one grant received would, at a minimum ($10,000), triple what I was asking the city to contribute.

I stated that our goal is to minimize the costs of other programs they are trying to fund. I stated if we could make a bathroom wheelchair accessible, a person may not have to move into their assisted housing program. If we could help re-train people to work, some even working from home, it would reduce the number of meals that would have to be delivered.

Just as importantly, each person we are able to get employed or qualified to receive disability payments, adds to the tax base as those funds will be spent in the local economy. The more funding we receive, the more employees we can hire, the more people we can help generate income, the more money goes into the tax base and generates sales taxes to help with their general fund.

I committed myself and our organization to the Council, stating that if I couldn't show I generated at least $6 for every dollar they provided, I would not ask for money the following year.

Unfortunately, by a split decision, the City Council voted against funding our organization that year.

Fortunately for us, it ended up being a blessing. One of the Council members asked me to stick around after the meeting was over. He had an idea.

The council member gave me the name of a local hotel manager. He felt the hotel manager would be able to assist us with fundraising.

On top of that, the President of the Police Officers Association, came up to me and stated, he liked the speech I gave and that the officers in attendance agreed that they would help raise $5,000 for our organization. They also offered to write letters in support of any federal grant we wanted to apply for to show local support.

Your Takeaways:

1. When asking for money, don't just focus on what you are doing to help those you serve. Focus on the benefits you are providing to the community at-large.

2. Don't be afraid to commit to a result in what you are doing. By showing confidence in what your organization will achieve, others will gain confidence in the organization.

3. Rejection or a denial doesn't mean they don't like your work or that what you do isn't valuable. It simply means they have more requests than means to fulfill all of them.

Action Steps:

1. Think of ways your organization benefits others besides those you serve directly. Begin to educate them on how they are benefitting and create allies.

2. Go back and talk to representatives of all governmental agencies, foundations, businesses or other funding sources, that liked what you do, but denied funding and see if they can provide referrals to other potential funding sources. Then follow-up!

Lesson # 2

Only Ask Others To Do, What You Do

I think almost every paid job I've had has provided an opportunity to use payroll deductions to give to the United Way, American Red Cross, or some other large non-profit organization.

I was still a teenager when I first committed to $25 a year to United Way. I got paid every two weeks and I agreed to contribute $1 a paycheck (actually ended up being $26, but what's a dollar).

With an organization like with United Way, you can select which organization you want your donation to go to and United Way will distribute their proceeds accordingly.

From the first non-profit organization I led and every one after that, I established an "Employee Payroll Contribution Program."

I used the following steps to introduce the program to the employees:

I began by asking if each employee had a favorite organization that they donated to. Almost everyone does. I then pointed out, if you work for an organization, you should believe in the work being done. If you are working for a worthy cause and you donate to worthy causes, why not donate to the one you work for?

I share it would be hard for me to ask others to donate to my organization, if I didn't donate. I inform them of my plan to go to local businesses in the communities we serve and ask them to establish an "Employee Payroll Contribution

Program" for our organization.

I share it would be just as hard for me to ask other companies to establish an Employee Payroll Contribution Plan, if our own organization doesn't have one.

I create payroll deduction forms for employees to fill out, indicating how much they want to deduct each pay period and have them submit it to the payroll department or whoever handles their payroll deductions, timesheets, etc.

I make it clear that it is truly a voluntary program. I don't look to see who is participating or how much they are participating. I do let the employees know how much I am contributing.

When I started this program for the first time, I contributed $1,000 for the year. We had 15 full-time employees. Combined, the total employee contribution plan equaled a little over $1,500.

After receiving permission to present the program to a local company's employees, I started by explaining the services we provided to local residents, how our services kept residents active in the community and contributing to the tax base.

Next, I would explain, their individual deductions would be combined and their employer would mail us one check each month for their total deductions.

Included with the check would be an itemized employee contribution list, stating the employees' names and the amount of their donations.

Their W-2 at the end of the year would list their contribution for their respective tax deductions.

I would be sure to let the employees know our own employees participate in a similar plan. I ask that they consider participating at a level they feel comfortable in giving. I point out that 100% of their contribution will stay in the county serving those in the local communities.

With my initial campaign, I said that "on average" our employees are each contributing $100 per year (15 employees and a total of $1,500).

I always invite those employees in attendance to come by our offices and meet staff. I encourage them to volunteer in some capacity as well so they can see firsthand the impact their time and donations have on those we serve.

While leading another organization, I challenged the staff to contribute $1,500 collectively. I agreed to match $1 for $1, up to $1,500 from my own paycheck. I assured them, I would ask the board of directors to match their contributions as well. I said with their $1,500 and my match of $1,500, I'd ask the board to match our total of $3,000.

Between the staff and myself, we reached the goal of $3,000 for the year.

Keeping my word, I presented the challenge to the board of directors. I ask that between them, to collectively match the $3,000 the staff was committing to the organization.

While the board didn't quite match the $3,000 goal, their cumulative pledges for the year exceeded the previous year.

I've been asked over the years how staff feel about having to contribute to their own place of business.

I make it clear that no one has to contribute. I make sure not to look at payroll deduction reports. I sincerely do not know which employees participate and which ones do not. It truly is a voluntary program.

Whether the individuals participate or not, the general consensus is they understand it would be difficult to ask individuals and businesses to set up contribution plans if we didn't have one of our own.

Without a doubt, employees like it when I say their contributions are considered "unrestricted" dollars, meaning the funds could be used for employee recognition, an office party, snacks, etc.

I think the best way to introduce any new program, project or procedure, is to be upfront and honest with all of the employees.

I share how the implementation will happen, providing timelines, etc.

I point out as many benefits to the employees as possible (if there are any).

Most importantly, I make sure their questions and concerns are addressed. If people feel like they are heard and acknowledged, most can handle what they may consider to be negative news or actions.

Your Takeaways:

1. Leading by example, doing first what you are asking others to do, shows it can be done. It shows your commitment and willingness to participate.

2. By acting first, you not only show others how to do something, you can leverage your participation, challenging others to match your commitment, and

combined, leverage the staff's participation to challenge the board of directors and local businesses.

3. By ensuring the local employees their contributions will stay in their communities, serving their neighbors, families and friends, gives your organization some leverage with the national and international non-profit organizations.

Action Steps:

1. If you don't already have an Employee Payroll Contribution Plan, get one started right away. It doesn't matter how many or how much you get in commitments. The point is to get started. The plan will grow over time.

2. Think of local area businesses, large and small, that you can present to the company and get their support. Most payroll processing companies can make the deductions, create the participant list and cut the check to your organization at little, if any, additional cost to the employer.

3. In making presentations to the local businesses, this is also a way to get them to connect with your purpose, mission and vision. So whether the company decides to participate right away or not, you're opening doors to educate them on what you do in the community, finding possible volunteers, and possible partners - not just sponsors.

Lesson # 3

Use Problems To Create Opportunities

It was an October Sunday morning, when I received a phone call from a concerned board member. It's not a good sign when a board member calls you on a Sunday.

He had just gotten off the phone with a friend, who happened to be a Regional Director for an organization, we had a subcontract with. She had expressed her displeasure with one of my management team who oversaw our portion of the contract. Our manager had been uncooperative and apparently was making negative comments about the lead organization.

I assured the concerned board member I would contact his friend the next morning and would keep him apprised of my progress in resolving the situation.

The following morning, I contacted the Regional Director and set up a time to meet for coffee, introduce myself, hear her concerns and discuss ways to resolve the situation.

When we met for coffee, she explained the situation and I assured her I would work on resolving the issues. I told her I felt one of my strengths was developing others. I would use this as an opportunity to demonstrate my abilities.

We shared our past experiences, what we enjoyed in our work and what we would like to develop in the future.

She oversaw prevention programs with her organization. I mentioned developing programs for a previous organization. I said I really enjoyed working with youth. I felt like our work with them was preventive. In trying to provide guidance to youth, it felt like we were on the proactive side of the pendulum, where with adults, we were on the reactive side.

I enjoyed putting energy and effort into trying to prevent youth from going down the wrong path as opposed to working with adults after the fact.

Our one hour meeting went almost two and a half hours. The majority of the time being spent on our visions for the future and exploring the possibilities of working together.

Prior to departing, she asked if I would be interested in bringing a youth program into our organization. She stated her organization was working on a grant proposal that would focus on educating 7th and 8th grade boys around gender respect. The ultimate goal being to stop teen dating violence before it begins.

Without hesitation, I said absolutely. Before saying good bye, she agreed to keep me posted on the grant process. I agreed to work on resolving the personnel issue.

Not long after the first of the year, she called to say her organization had received the youth grant. She said there would be a three-day training in March. The training, hotel, food & travel costs would be paid for. I would only have to commit to attending all 3 days. I committed on the spot.

From our initial meeting to when the training was going to be held was about four and a half months. During that time, I worked with the Manager to resolve the conflict. Luckily, the issue did not come up again.

During the two months leading up to the training, I apprised the board of directors of this new program we would be implanting in the community. We would be training adult volunteers to act as co-facilitators to educate boys in after-school programs, at our offices, and other community locations.

With anything new, there will always be some resistance, some negative feedback. This was no exception.

One of the more vocal, outspoken board members didn't like the idea of starting something new. He worried about staff being stretched too thin. He felt the program wasn't in line with our mission statement.

I quickly pointed out that the program would be run by volunteers, that it would not affect the workload of current staff, other than myself. I explained that since part of our mission was to create a safe environment suitable for family lifestyle, reducing or eliminating teen dating violence would fall under creating a safe environment.

Still dissatisfied, he accused me of "chasing money." I assured him that nothing could be further from the truth. He asked me to explain. I said because I didn't know if there was any funding in the program for us. I said that funding was never part of our discussions.

Then he wanted to know why I agreed to do the program. I simply said because it was the right thing to do. It would benefit the community.

I attended the training. While there, I developed relationships with members of other organizations that continue to this day.

After the training was completed, I was able to recruit 13 adult volunteers that went through a training-for trainers and then several of them paired up as co-facilitators to begin offering the program at our main location and a couple assisted in offering the program at an after-school program held on campus at one of the public schools.

There actually was no funding for our organization in offering this program. However, as you'll see in some of the other lessons, this program did lead to funding.

Your Takeaways:

1. When faced with a problem, look at it as an opportunity to grow from. In searching for a solution, keep your eyes and ears open for opportunities to connect with others. You may recognize similar dreams, visions, and opportunities to do something with others.

2. Every business, every organization has problems. There will always be customer complaints and dissatisfied clients. These are opportunities for you and your organization to shine. Solving a problem, creates more than a satisfied customer or client, it creates a grateful one! These are the ones that want to come back and do business with you. They are the ones that speak the highest compliments.

3. You will always face opposition. Regardless of the need you are trying to fill, the good you are trying to do, there will always be opposition. Know your values ahead of time. Know what you are trying to accomplish. Do not let naysayers destroy what you are trying to accomplish.

4. There is no reward in maintaining the status quo.

Action Steps:

1. Look at problems you are currently facing or ones you've recently overcome. Instead of getting rid of the problem, look to see if there are opportunities to build something from the problem.

2. Analyze the problems you are facing now. Determine if the problems are indicators that you should be doing things differently, more efficiently, or maybe you should be doing completely different things.

3. After the first two action steps, if you think there may be opportunities, or ways to do things differently, more efficiently, or possibly there may be other things you should be doing, take action and implement your ideas. Evaluate the progress, the feedback and determine if you need to make adjustments or continue the action you are taking.

4. Remember, without a different perspective, without taking different steps, you will continue to see the same path, continue taking the same steps, and continue getting the same results.

Lesson # 4

Connected Donors Become Partners

Having led multiple non-profits, each serving different populations, one of the most frustrating things in dealing with funding sources is they change their focus from time to time, causing organizations to change or lose funding.

For example if a foundation is focused on employment services and then decides to change their focus to senior services, you can see the negative effect it could have on an organization providing employment services.

One organization I led held an annual Health Fair. We collaborated with health care providers, chiropractors, civic organizations and others to offer free medical screenings, eye tests, etc., to local residents. Other local community based organizations passed out brochures and information on the services they offered as well. We even had a bicycle safety course for younger children and provided free bicycle helmets to participants.

Over the years, a local foundation had consistently provided a check for $2,000 to help with the cost of the health fair.

After experiencing the 2nd health fair during my employment, I decided to reach out to the grant manager of this local foundation with a Letter of Inquiry (LOI).

I began by thanking the foundation for their continuing support. I summarized our existing service components to promote change in the community.

I also included a vision for some programs we were looking to implement. I explained I was looking for partnerships. I wanted to find foundations, businesses, and other donors that would come and see the work we do, get a sense of what we are trying to accomplish, and see the real needs of those we serve. I said if a potential funder felt a connection and believed in what we were doing, I would ask them to partner with us and make a three-year funding commitment.

I invited him to come by the office for coffee, to learn more about our vision and to see if the foundation would be interested in making a $15,000 contribution to get one of the new programs started and to consider a three-year commitment.

It took nearly two months before I received a phone call from this foundation's fund manager. He said he appreciated the invitation. He wasn't sure if what we were doing matched up with the foundation's mission.

He was intrigued by one of our existing components, the Neighborhood Action Teams (NATs). He wanted to know if he could come by and observe a couple of the meetings.

I sent him the meeting schedule of each Neighborhood Action Team and the focus of each team.

After coming by and meeting me, I introduced him to several of the NAT facilitators. He observed several meetings. He told me he enjoyed the teams and admired the teams' desire to improve their neighborhood. He liked the platform because he felt it was building leaders in the community.

He asked me what type of commitment I was looking for. I explained I didn't have an all-or-nothing platform. I admitted this was a new concept and since his foundation was local and had provided consistent support for the Health Fair over the years, I was starting with him.

My initial request for a $15,000 donation was to operate one of the new programs for a year. I said it would be great if the foundation would make a 3-year commitment to fund an entire program and pick a date for payment each year, or if they preferred, they could pay out quarterly. If not, funding part of a program would still be appreciated. I was mostly interested in a buy-in, a commitment to the cause.

He said he would take the idea and what he had experienced and share the information with the founders.

Almost three months later, without even a phone call, I received a letter from the fund manager stating the founders liked the neighborhood program concept. They enclosed a check for $10,000.

It was a beginning. The letter didn't contain any reporting requirements or restrictions on the funds. There wasn't a commitment to an extended period of time. It confirmed to me, I was on the right track.

Your Takeaways:

1. To stand out from other applicants, where everyone is evaluated on the grant writer's skills, to be looked upon as something more than an organization with it's hand out, there can be long-term benefits by establishing a connection with the foundation and its decision-makers.

2. Whether it's a business, a foundation, or donors, if you can get them to connect with your organization on a personal level, you can get long-term buy-in, long-term commitment.

3. When donors can see the need, see the difference

your organization is making, see the impact their contribution is having on those being served, the donor will **feel** their importance, **feel** the difference they are making and likely want to contribute more.

Action Steps:

1. Look through your funding sources, your donor lists, and start inviting them to visit your organization. Get them to see those committed to serving your clients. Let them talk with clients and hear first hand how the services are helping them and their families.

2. Look at businesses, individuals and foundations that have made it known they support the type of work your organization is doing and connect with them. Share with them a vision of how what you are doing will fulfill their desire to make a difference.

3. Ask how your organization could be a benefit, a good partner, a good neighbor for a local business, a large donor, a local foundation. Then take massive action to become that benefit, partner and neighbor. The support you'll receive will exceed what you hope for.

Lesson # 5

By Offering More Value, You Increase Revenues

All businesses, non-profits, community based organizations, and other entities focus their work on their direct end-user, consumer or client.

There are other ways to add value to others.

Our organization had an office centrally located in the county. We had ample parking and a large conference room that for the most part went unused.

While attending a Senior Mobility meeting put on by the county's Aging & Adult Services Department, the leaders were discussing their efforts to find a centrally located place for their next meeting.

I offered the use of our conference room. They asked if it would be okay to make it a brown bag lunch meeting. I assured them it wouldn't be a problem.

The initial meeting was successful and I agreed to host future meetings. The meetings were attended by representatives from multiple organizations and governmental entities.

With the offering of our conference room, immediately at least a dozen organizations became aware of our organization, the services we offered, in addition to our location.

We immediately began to get new referrals. With some of our funding tied to the number of clients served, this would be a long-term benefit for our organization.

After a few months of meetings, one of the county department heads asked me if I was interested in collaborating with them on a grant proposal. He knew a foundation that was interested in funding "demonstration grants." It would be a one-year grant to demonstrate a theory. We would have to present a theory, show how it would work, and then, explain how it would continue once the funding ended.

I told him we would love to participate as long as the grant included the populations we served.

We ended up collaborating on a grant proposal we called "Mobility for Independence Program (M4IP)."

We would collaborate with Aging & Adult Services and the central county bus service to demonstrate if a senior citizen and/or person with a disability had available transportation to get to the doctor's, pharmacy and grocery store, they could continue to live independently.

We would use the grant funds to print tickets and passes for the bus routes and wheelchair accessible mini-trucks that would pick up individual passengers at their home and drop them off at their specific destinations (in the same manner as taxicabs).

The drivers of the bus service would track the pick up and drop off locations of each participant.

At the end of the funding period, we proposed we would go to the grocery stores, pharmacies and other locations the passengers frequented and let them know they had "X" number of customers, patients, etc., due to their access to transportation. We would ask for contributions from these business establishments to help with on-going funding.

In addition, we would ask the respective cities that the participants resided in to contribute a portion of their fine money from illegally parked vehicles in parking stalls reserved for individuals with disabilities to go towards future program costs.

We were able to receive a $20,000 grant for this demonstration project.

This funding, the increased referrals to our program, the relationships with other organizations and county departments, as well as the business owners and the county bus personnel all came about by simply offering the use of an empty conference room.

Your Takeaways:

1. Regardless of the type of business you are in, there is something you can offer to others that doesn't directly affect the gross receipts, but indirectly can affect much more.

2. Every business can offer a service of some type that will start with increased awareness and relationship building. All business is relationships.

3. The work you do, the services you provide, have ripple effects beyond your immediate customer or client.

Action Items:

1. Think about who can benefit from the use of your conference room, parking lot, or maybe you have an extra office or idle time your receptionist, accountant, etc., that could benefit someone else.

2. Think about after work. Maybe you could provide access after business hours for a community meeting, A.A. or N.A. meeting, where your next superstar could come from.

3. Think about a service you offer that would be a good fit for another business or another industry that you could leverage.

Lesson # 6

It's Amazing What You Can Accomplish If You Don't Care Who Gets The Credit

While serving as the Executive Director for an organization, who's mission was to help individuals with disabilities to live as independently as possible, I received a phone call from a woman wanting to donate a battery-powered wheelchair. Her husband had bought it new. She explained he had recently passed away. Until his death, she said the wheelchair was like a gift from heaven. It allowed them to spend their last few years together traveling and enjoying life.

Since she no longer had a use for the wheelchair, she wanted to make sure someone else could benefit from it. Her only requirement was she drove a compact car and it wouldn't fit in her vehicle. Someone would have to pick it up. She said to make sure two people came as the wheelchair was heavy.

I thanked her and assured her I would make arrangements to pick up the wheelchair and have it delivered to someone that would benefit from its use.

I shared this information with my staff. The staff began to think of their consumers and which one would like the powered wheelchair the most.

I told them, I had an idea, where I thought not only would the end-user benefit, but our organization and others could benefit as well. I received several puzzled looks.

We were in the process of deciding what type of fundraiser we wanted to put on since the organization had relied completely on governmental funding until I had arrived. I felt we needed to expand revenue streams and increase the public's awareness of our existence.

Most community organizations such as Lions Clubs, Rotary Clubs, Kiwanis Clubs, Soroptimist Clubs and others are skilled fundraisers. They continually raise money for their mission and activities.

I had recently spoken with a Rotarian about ideas for a fundraiser. He had provided several types of events we could put on, giving us the pros and cons to each type of event. He happen to be the general manager of a hotel and offered the use of the hotel to hold whichever type of event we decided on.

Since our organization provided services to residents in two counties, we had multiple offices in several cities across the two counties.

In one city, the organization had maintained an office for almost 10 years with a staff of 6-8 full-time employees. The city had initially provided an annual grant of $1,000-$1,500. After 3-4 years, the funding had stopped.

In my first year as the Executive Director of the organization, I submitted a grant proposal and spoke before Grant Selection Committee as well as the City Council on why the organization should be funded. We were denied again.

I told the staff, we could use the wheelchair to help someone in need, the Rotary Club, and the City Council. Again, I received more puzzled looks.

I suggested we let the Rotary Club select someone they knew in need in their community and we would let them present the wheelchair to the individual, with the stipulation, we invite the mayor of the city to be present and a local reporter for the local newspaper.

I explained we would be able to say that in collaboration with the local Rotary Club, we were happy to provide the wheelchair to one of their supporters/members. We could credit the Mayor and the City Council for their years of support (although they weren't funding us). It was through their leadership that organizations such as ours and the Rotary Club were able to contribute and support the local community.

I believed by giving value to the Rotary Club first, they would help us even more that we would hope for in future fundraising. I believed by giving the mayor and the city council some value first, through positive press coverage (politicians like photo ops), they might look favorably on our next grant proposal. I believed another benefit would be notifying the local reporter about a positive news story. By giving him the advance notice, and a chance to get a byline in the paper, I believed down the road, when we were looking for some positive press, he would be inclined to give it to us, since we benefitted him first.

Whether the Rotary Club would work harder to help us in the future or whether the City Council would support us through a future grant or whether we could expect future press coverage, couldn't be assured. Furthermore, it shouldn't be expected.

I believe as a community based organization, we should be helping as many people and organizations as possible. I understand and recognize grant funding dollars have restrictions, but as you can see above, the benefits we would be providing cost absolutely nothing and the relationship building could provide long-term values.

Your Takeaways:

1. Whenever you are receiving a benefit, a donation, press coverage, or doing a good deed for someone or the community you serve, use the opportunity to benefit others in the process.

2. By recognizing the good that others are doing in the community you serve, will get others to recognize the good you are doing without you having to toot your own horn.

Action Steps:

1. Figure out what organizations, businesses, and individuals can you recognize, praise, and support - whether they have ever helped you or not - and begin adding value now.

2. Develop a column in your newsletter, on your website, or send out a regular press release highlighting someone or an organization doing something positive in the community that is unrelated to your organization.

Lesson # 7

If You Want Others To Contribute, Contribute To Others

The topic of discussion is a faint memory as I remember standing in the reception area with a few employees and a couple of consumers when the phone rang. We became silent, as we listened to half of a conversation. It wasn't long before I heard my cue, "One moment please. I'll put you through and he'll be right with you."

My extension was just beginning to ring as I sat at my desk and answered the phone. As I said hello, I could hear shallow breathing as a woman proceeded to share a life changing experience. Her husband had recently had a stroke and was going to be released from the hospital in a day or two. He was no longer able to walk. She was in need of a wheelchair and could not afford to buy one. She wanted to know if we had wheelchairs available for these type of situations.

I shared with her, I was new to the organization. It was my second week and I didn't know for sure. I told her, I would find her a wheelchair. I assured her, it would be in her husband's best interests, as well as her own, to focus her energy on him and leave the acquisition of a wheelchair to me.

I took her information and promised to get back to her with an update within 24 hours.

While my mind was spinning thinking about whether I had any contacts at some of the local churches and/or other local organizations that may be able to contribute a wheelchair through a member of their respective congregations, I went in to share the situation with my top two managers.

While I may have just started, they were experienced, having been with the organization seven years and fourteen years respectively.

Much to my surprise, I was informed we not only had a new wheelchair available to give away, but we had five new wheelchairs.

I asked where we got the wheelchairs and when did we get them.

The wheelchairs were provided by the Wheelchair Foundation (www.wheelchairfoundation.org), a non-profit organization with a goal to provide a free wheelchair to every child, teen and adult worldwide who needs one, but has no means to acquire one.

The Wheelchair Foundation is an incredible organization, doing incredible things. A wonderful story for another book.

Our organization had been blessed to be the recipient of these five wheelchairs. These wheelchairs had sat in an office, unused for over a year.

Bewildered, I asked why the wheelchairs had not been distributed to people in need. I was told because no one had asked for a wheelchair. I asked if we had advertised them as being available. They had not.

I pointed out, if no one knew we had wheelchairs available, no one would ever ask us for a wheelchair.

Having only been with the organization for two weeks, I was beginning to understand why the funding streams had been limited to just federal funding that was mandated through the American with Disabilities Act.

No one within the organization was ever taught that by giving value first, when it comes time to ask for help, you'll receive more than you could hope for.

In a short period of time, it became crystal clear, we needed to reach out to other organizations, businesses, etc.

The majority of individuals with disabilities and their families were unaware of our organization and the services we offered that were available to them.

I suggested that we contact all of the churches in the area and let them know we had a few wheelchairs available for anyone in their respective congregations that may need one.

I suggested we let other non-profit organizations know as well, in case someone they served needed a wheelchair.

This was a great training opportunity for staff. I was able to teach them by offering other organizations, what we had available to us, later on, when we had a need for one of our clients, they would likely try to assist us.

I explained this is how collaborations begin. This is how we add value to other organizations. This is how we really impact the communities we serve.

I shared that even if none of the churches or organizations had anyone that could benefit from a free, new wheelchair, they would all know we were thinking of them and trying to assist someone they served.

As we provided a wheelchair to the woman who initially called me, we made a point to acknowledge the Wheelchair

Foundation made the donation possible. I made sure we would acknowledge the generous donation and share the work of the Wheelchair Foundation with each recipient of the four remaining wheelchairs.

Your Takeaways:

1. By offering assistance to other organizations serving various populations, you increase the amount of assistance that will be offered to you - whether anyone accepts your offer to help or not.

2. There is no easier way or cost effective way to get the word out about the good your organization is doing than by offering your services or a helping hand to leaders of other organizations.

Action Steps:

1. Think about the population you serve. Identify other organizations, businesses, clubs, etc., that those you serve may frequent or participate in. Reach out to those organizations, businesses, and clubs, offering your services to any of their clients that may be in need.

2. Think about items or other offerings you have available to give to someone that could benefit, but are just sitting around. Figure out ways to offer them to organizational leaders, that can spread the word for you, and receive some of the credit for getting the items or other offerings to those that can benefit from them right now.

Lesson # 8

Do The Work And The Money Will Come

This is a concept many individuals and organizations find difficult to believe. It's even harder to put into action. This is where your faith comes into play.

From the time we are an employee working for someone else, we hear people say, "they don't pay me enough to do that" or "That's not in my job description." Organizations will say, "we don't have the funds for that or we don't have the staffing."

You cannot tell a fireplace to give you heat and then you'll put a log on. You have to start the fire first and then feel the warmth.

You have to put in the work and then your efforts will be recognized for the promotion or pay raise.

Some organizational leaders fear starting something of value that meets a need. This may be due to lack of confidence or having the vision to see the opportunities in problems that can lead to funding.

Some leaders only see the increase in their work load, or the additional work for staff. They cannot visualize their abilities to increase funding and employment opportunities, thereby increasing their services.

Then there are those with a feeling of entitlement. These individuals think they should be paid more first. These are the ones that spend their entire careers complaining about being overworked and underpaid. They complain about others being lucky or only getting promoted because they're related to the owner, or countless other reasons. The only reason they leave out is that they worked harder.

As I mentioned previously in Lesson # 3, "Use Problems to Create Opportunities", I once had a board member accuse me of "chasing money." Nothing could be further from the truth.

The previous experience I shared regarding agreeing to add the youth program tailored for 7th and 8th grade boys, educating them on gender respect with the goal of preventing teen dating violence, without the promise of any funding is a good example of Lesson # 8, "Do the work and the money will come."

While I was at the initial 3-day youth program training-for-trainers, the collaborating organization contacted me regarding our interest in another possible collaboration.

This project would be funded by the U.S. Dept. of Justice (Office on Violence Against Women) and was for two-years totaling $300,000 ($150,000/year).

The project would be to help immigrant women that were victims of domestic violence.

The project would require a community based organization to be the lead agency and to collaborate with another agency with clinical experience to provide the clinical counseling services.

As the community based organization, we would need to provide a group meeting place and hire a full-time "Promotora" (a Latino outreach worker in the Latino community responsible for raising awareness of the services available and using trust and rapport to help the abused women seek counseling and other services).

As the lead agency, we would be responsible for the required reporting and the funds would be distributed to us.

I agreed to the collaborative effort.

I suggested, since their agency would be providing the clinical skills associated with the program, they should receive the majority of the funding, if awarded. They countered that we should receive the larger portion of the proceeds.

At the time we submitted the proposal, the budget indicated our organization would receive about 60% of the funds.

At the next board meeting, I apprised my board of directors of the pending collaborative grant application. This time a naysayer questioned why I agreed to the grant proposal. They informed me they had applied with the same organization on the same grant before and were denied.

I explained that I didn't know of the past experiences or why the proposal was rejected. I did say that past results don't have to equal future results. Proposals may be worded differently. The funding source may have more funds to distribute or less applications.

There were too many variables to list them all. One thing is for sure, you should not base your future actions on past results.

Just because one diet didn't help you lose weight doesn't mean another diet won't give you different results.

Timing, motivation, targeted geographic areas are all factors that play into funding decisions especially on a national scale.

We were awarded the two-year grant for $300,000, spread out over the two-year period.

In addition to being awarded the grant, we were connected with a nationally recognized organization headquartered in Minnesota, that provided training, mentoring, etc. This additional bonus was instrumental in the growth of the staff we assigned to the program as well as our management team.

This was the first federal grant awarded to our agency in its 10+ years history. It was also our first multi-year grant.

While obvious, it is worth stating, multi-year grants provide stability and extend credibility to an organization and the work it is doing in the community.

So, after initially trying to resolve a personnel issue, I'm grateful to say, I was able to position our organization to collaborate on a grant that resulted in zero funding - but brought a quality program to the community we served. From that zero funded grant, we were able to collaborate on our organization's first multi-year grant and first federal grant.

Your Takeaways:

1. By doing the right things for the right reasons, money will come to you. It may not come as expected, but rewards come in many ways.

2. True collaborations start before funding arrives. If you reach out to other organizations and share a common vision, both sides will look for ways to work together.

3. A key component to collaborating is putting forth effort to ensure the other agency gets what they want and to offer as much credit and recognition to them as possible. In doing so, you'll find you receive more funding, get more credit and receive more recognition, than if you had sat at a table and tried to negotiate them.

Action Steps:

1. Identify organizations or businesses in your community that your work can compliment their work and/or their mission.

2. Meet with their leadership and see if there are ways your organization can help them or work with them at no cost to them. Your initial efforts should be for the sole purpose of benefitting their organization and those they serve.

3. Instead of chasing funds in numerous areas, continue to focus on doing what you do best, invest in building relationships and using your organization's strengths to generate funding opportunities.

Lesson # 9

If Meetings Are A Must, Bring A Must To The Meetings

Meetings, meetings, meetings. I'm a person that dreads attending most meetings. Meetings can be very time consuming and very costly. Most meetings are very unproductive.

What makes most meetings fall into these unfavorable categories is they are held as a standard practice and generally are meant to disseminate information one-way, from the top down.

Meetings that are held as a standard of practice, eventually gets to the point where the person conducting the meeting has to look for things to include on the agenda. This is when you really know a standard meeting has outlived its purpose and value.

Meetings can be very beneficial and productive. Networking meetings or meetings that provide time to network among those in attendance can be extremely beneficial if the right strategy is in place.

I've gone to work with organizations and consulted with numerous others and found the reason or reasons used for staff attending meetings outside of the office are off the charts.

Sometimes an employee will be assigned to attend a community based meeting and will have attended the same monthly meeting for years. They don't contribute at the meeting, they don't know all of those in attendance, they don't bring back any pertinent information to benefit the organization they are representing and when asked, aren't really sure why they attend. It's become part of the job duties.

If an organization is going to hold a regular meeting, if only one person is going to share information, it can be handled by email or voice mail. At least this way, employees don't have to postpone productive work to learn something they can get by reading or listening to at their convenience.

When preparing to attend a meeting, an individual, regardless of position within an organization, should know which individuals will likely be in attendance. Each individual should have pre-set goals. The first goal would be to meet two new individuals and learn what they are doing and what they are looking for to grow their respective organization. The second goal should be to find two people you know that have not met and introduce them to one another. This will give you an opportunity to edify both parties with no ulterior motive. That's it.

You want to save what you are doing, what your organization has accomplished for individual follow-up afterwards.

The exception to this rule is if you are there to make a big announcement pertaining to your organization.

When you do talk about the work you are doing, the success you are having, whether it's in the individual follow-up contacts or during a networking interaction, spend most of the time talking about the success of others. If you're in a collaboration, share how wonderful it is to work with the staff, the commitment they bring to the table. Let those listening hear how much you appreciate the others involved in whatever you are discussing.

If it's a program within your own organization, discuss the success of your staff, those that influenced your ability to start the program, etc.

By spending time talking about others, those listening will soon realize, if they worked with you or for you, you would talk about them the same way!

I was blessed to meet a woman that spear-headed an on-going collaborative effort of bringing multiple organizations, members of school districts, therapists, and others interested in stopping domestic violence together. The collaborative met to share ideas, best practices, to learn what other resources were available, to get to know others that shared in the passion of creating safe environments for children and to improve families.

I was able to share with the group, the awarding of our federal grant to help immigrant women that were victims of domestic violence. (See Lesson # 8.)

I shared how wonderful it was working with our collaborative partner in both the promoting gender respect program for middle school age boys and now this two-year grant.

I expanded on how wonderful the Minnesota organization was that was hired to educate, train and mentor the awardees in this round of funding.

I shared how the Minnesota organization had started a Campaign for Hope, asking individuals to sign a declaration stating they would stand with others to create a world free from domestic violence by grounding my relationships (of all kinds) in love, respect and understanding.

I had contacted the organization and asked if we could duplicate their model and use it on the west coast. They were so willing and helpful. They sent us free videos that we could post on our website.

I mentioned to the group, how I would love for our male volunteers to go out into the community and establish some men groups that could start our own Hope Campaign, going door-to-door, educating others on how stopping domestic violence is a men's issue and how if we educate young boys before they become men that hitting a woman was not acceptable at any time, we can stop unnecessary violence before it happens.

It wasn't long after that, the woman that spear-headed this group, who I now consider a friend and one of my mentors, contacted me to discuss my dream of creating the local Hope Campaign.

She asked me to draft up a proposal on how I would implement it, what it would cost to complete the project, and the phases from starting to finish.

In a nutshell, I suggested that we would start with small groups of men, willing to hold community meetings in apartment complexes, churches, school yards, etc. Those educated and willing would team up in groups of 2 or 3 and systematically go door-to-door down one street, block-to-block, neighborhood to neighborhood, getting declarations signed by the men and women living in those areas.

While getting the declarations signed, the men would also be creating support systems, exchanging contact information, so they would have others to call when they started to feel anger or frustration.

I included dreams of recognition. I thought once we had 90% of a block with signed declarations, we could declare it a "Violence Free Zone." Just like neighborhoods and schools have "Drug Free Zone" signs, we could do the same on the residential streets. Potential new residents would know that violence wasn't tolerated in their community.

I made the assumption, "Violence Free Zones" would eventually improve property values as well. Everyone wants to live in safe, friendly areas that are suitable for healthy lifestyles.

I thought it would be great to hold a block-party, with city officials there to put the sign in the ground and have a band play to celebrate the neighborhood's commitment to end violence.

My hope was the publicity and social-proof would create momentum.

The organization my friend and mentor ran awarded our organization a $20,000 grant to implement the Campaign for Hope.

This all began by participating in a non-funded collaborative group from all sectors across a county to stop domestic violence.

It was the shared passion and expression of being blessed to work with other outstanding organizations, that brought this funding to our organization.

Your Takeaways:

1. By spreading positive words about the work others are doing, by giving others accolades for the contributions they have made to your success, you

are benefitting them and your organization simultaneously. As your compliments and expressed gratitude makes them look good, it makes others want to work with you because they know you say positive things about those you collaborate with.

2. By talking about the incredible work other organizations are doing; their willingness to allow you to duplicate their efforts; their eagerness to train your staff; and the benefits you received from the shortened learning curve, helps validate the work you are doing.

3. By focusing on others, asking about their programs, philosophies, their dreams and plans for accomplishing them, shows others you care about them. No one cares about how much you know, until they know how much you care.

Action Steps:

1. Create a list of meetings, the staff members that attend, and the purpose of each meeting.

2. Meet with staff members to create goals for each meeting and follow-up protocol.

3. Role play with staff on how they can edify others working with the organization as well as those working within the organization.

4. Spend time with staff discussing ways to share positive experiences working with other organizations, members of the community, with other entities.

LESSON # 10

Solving A Problem Generates More Funds Than Complaining

During an election year, while serving as the Executive Director for Independent Living Resource .of Contra Costa County, advocates for individuals with disabilities brought to my attention, complaints of an insufficient number of accessible voting sites.

I had no clue what the requirements were to qualify as a Polling Center. I didn't know what, if any, accommodations were available for individuals with disabilities.

I sat down with my management team to learn more about the lack of accessible sites and accessible voting equipment.

The general consensus I got was the Registrar of Voters Office was aware of the need for more accessible poll centers, not just locally, but everywhere. My management team felt little or nothing was being done about it   If progress was being made, it was coming so slowly, it didn't appear to be moving.

I asked if any of my predecessors had talked to the Registrars of Voters for our county. They didn't believe so. I asked if any of them had contacted the county office. None of the current staff had spoken with anyone from the Registrar's Office.

Our organization had been in its current location for almost 6 years. We had more than the required designated handicap parking stalls. We had a large conference room. It was obvious to me, we were accessible, as many of our consumers were in wheelchairs, as well as some of our staff and volunteers. Our bathrooms were accessible and the ramp to the front door from the parking lot was used on a daily basis by multiple individuals using wheelchairs.

I had an idea and put it out there for the management team to consider. I asked, why not use our conference room for a Poll Center? If there weren't enough accessible sites, instead of complaining, let's become one.

The team was surprised. The thought had never come up before. They were excited about the possibility of being able to offer more accessibility to voters.

I contacted the County's Registrar's Office. I spoke directly to the Registrar. She was extremely cooperative. She was aware of the need for more accessibility. She indicated her staff were always on the lookout for accessible and available sites to operate as a Polling Center.

She explained how the process worked for becoming a site. She stated an inspector would visit the site and take measurements to determine accessibility.

She said even though we served consumers needing accessibility to buildings, their protocol required the site visit.

She also explained to me a program available to non-profit organizations called "Adopt-A-Poll." She asked me if we would be interested in participating. I responded with a quick "absolutely."

The Adopt-A-Poll Program basically allows a non-profit to earn up to $800 per election for hosting and staffing a Poll Center on Election Day.

The $800 could be partially earned as there was an itemized list of things required to host and operate a Poll Center.

The Lead Person would have to attend a training on how to control the ballots, what to do if a machine jammed, where to deliver the ballots afterwards, etc.

There was a dollar amount attached to each volunteer that worked a shift. There was a fixed amount for rent of the location, and so forth.

I was thrilled to learn, not only could we help reduce the accessibility problem, but we could earn almost a thousand dollars in the process.

I felt this solution would bring an added bonus. In one of our grants, a goal we had each year was to increase the number of registered voters.

I felt with the excitement of becoming a Poll Center, it would help to remind everyone to encourage all of the consumers that weren't registered to vote, to complete the voter registration card and we would ensure it was mailed in.

I was shocked a few days later, when I received a phone call from the Registrar. She told me our facility didn't qualify as an accessible building. Evidently, the ramp from the parking lot to the front door was 1 or 2 degrees too steep to qualify.

I wasn't sure what to say. How could the ramp be used daily by so many without complaint or difficulty and it still not be in compliance.

One of our staff, consulting on the side with contractors regarding American with Disabilities Act (ADA) requirements, personally used the ramp multiple times on a daily basis without any difficulty.

I was starting to think, no wonder it's difficult to find accessible sites.

The Registrar told me we could still be a site. She indicated we would need to have an ambulatory individual available the entire time the poll center was open to assist with pushing wheelchairs up the ramp as well as assist going down the ramp.

I assured her we would.

Election Day came and went without incident. The Registrar's Office mailed us a check for the full $800.

It was a great learning experience for all of us. I think of the 16 people that participated in working shifts, I believe only 1 had prior experience as a Poll Worker.

What was really surprising and an unexpected benefit was the number of voters that came in, totally unaware of our existence.

Many voters took time to look at our brochures. Several had questions answered about elderly relatives and resources available to them.

Over the next year, several voters came by and dropped off donations. A few became volunteers.

I know at least two of the volunteers attended an Open House and shared the joy they experienced volunteering with our staff and consumers.

Your Takeaways:

1. This is a classic example of "if you're not part of the solution, you're part of the problem."
2. If you focus your energies on solutions instead of complaining and waiting for others to solve the

problem, everything is possible.

3. By reaching out and offering to be a partner in the solution long-term relationships are established and collaborations come to life.

4. Organizing others to complain, protest, and hold hearings wastes energy, resources and destroys goodwill.

Action Steps:

1. Make a list of on-going problems, complaints, and concerns you receive as they pertain to other businesses, organizations, as well as those pertaining to your organization.

2. Next to each item on the list, think about what you and the organization can do to help resolve the problem, complaint or concern.

3. Contact a representative of those other businesses, organizations and the management representative in your own organization responsible for the department receiving negative remarks and schedule a meeting or time for a call to discuss ideas on how to resolve the on-going issues. Explain your goal is not to reiterate the problems and to be part of the solution.

4. At the meeting, figure out what you and your organization can do to solve the problem. The solutions should be offered without expectation of compensation or reimbursement. Have faith, that if there is funding available to offset any costs, it will be offered.

If no compensation results from resolving the problems,

realize the relationship and bond you built during the solution process, will come back tenfold to you and your organization.

It may or may not come from the same organization. However, it will come from someone discovering what you did for the other organization, or from a collaborative grant that can be traced back to your good will.

Lesson #11

Use Creativity To Grow Your Funds

By purposely thinking about how to bring recognition to others, you will discover incredible opportunities to increase the recognition of your business.

I applied to become the Executive Director of an organization focused on improving an entire community because I wanted to work with all segments, all entities that make a community whole.

I was excited about the possibilities of organizing the four hundred plus businesses in the geographic area the organization served.

From my first day on the job my message was clear. I believed if we provided value to the businesses first, when we needed contributions, we would receive more than if we showed up with our hand out, having to explain who we were and what we were trying to accomplish.

One example came after I secured our office as a designated site for a Volunteer Income Tax Assistance (VITA) Program.

With VITA, low income residents could get their taxes prepared and filed for free at our office through volunteers that signed up to help prepare them. Site managers received free training from the Internal Revenue Service.

In an effort to market the local businesses, I sent them an email explaining that many local residents, their target market, would be filing their income tax returns at our office.

I offered to make coupons for their business, at no cost to

them, to give to those completing their tax returns.

I asked that they email me a business logo to put on the coupon, as well as whatever they wanted to offer.

I assured them, I would send a draft of the coupon back for their approval before distributing them.

A couple of suggestions I made were "bring this coupon stamped by the location filing your tax return and receive a free tire rotation" "bring this coupon stamped by the location filing your tax return and receive a free cup of coffee with the purchase of a pastry."

Whether the coupons were used or not, individuals would learn about the business or be reminded of the business.

Unlike paying for an ad in the newspaper or on the internet, where it could receive a million views but only twenty five were in the market area, one hundred percent of those receiving a coupon would live or work in the market area.

Whether the coupons were used or not, whether a business participated or not, they all knew I was trying to provide value to their respective business by giving them exposure.

Another example came while working for the same organization, trying to assist the same business community.

During the taking of the U.S. Census, I volunteered our offices for Census takers to be available for questions from the community.

As the census taking period was about to come to a close, we received a small grant to host a community event with the theme "California Stand and Be Counted."

The grant was to be used for prizes, advertising, etc., in an effort to get people out, ensure they were counted and included in the U.S. Census.

We coordinated the use of a local school's auditorium, providing them a rental fee.

We hired a local business that offered blow-up rooms for kids to jump in.

We invited all of the non-profits that served the community to have a free table at the event to educate the community of the services they offer.

We had T-shirts printed with "I love to shop at" on the front and randomly picked 75 local businesses to list on the back to use as door prizes.

As you can see from one small grant, we were able to financially benefit a school, a local business, and market 75 specific businesses as well as the entire community.

Social media is another simple way to provide value and recognition to others that can benefit you and your organization in the long run.

As an example, picture a local community based organization serving residents within a three square mile area.

You could send volunteers door to door to acquire email addresses and cell phone numbers to let the community know, you will notify them when local stores have sales or promotions. You can ask them to visit your website to acquire additional information.

You do the same things with all the businesses within the

area that serve directly to those living in the three square mile area.

You inform the businesses that you have a database with contact information of their target market.

You can provide free marketing for those businesses and simply state over time, you'd like them to contribute to your organization, in the amount they feel they received value for.

Now, instead of paying huge amounts for radio, TV and newspaper ads, that covers a larger audience, but not specific to the business target market, each business receives value, because they don't pay for something that might not give a return.

As the returns come in, they will gladly contribute more than you would've expected to receive and they will probably endorse you on grant opportunities. It's a win-win that others aren't offering them.

Some good examples include:

Using Twitter, tweet an announcement to your database "Stop by Joe's carwash today and mention ABC Co. and receive $3 off your wash." Joe gets free advertising, and some extra cars come in on a slow day, where he's paying washers either way.

Another tweet might be: "It's late, no time to cook tonight? Order from Sue's Pizza 555-555-5555, mention ABC Co & get $2 off."

The best part of these examples, is they can be done on five minutes notice. This is a huge benefit for Joe and for Sue. Slow nights, immediate results.

You can ask businesses to provide coupons that can be printed online that you can post on your website along with a link to their company website listed under "community partner or support."

Some may offer a prize for checking your website often. You can have enter daily for a chance to win a 2 for 1 dinner at Patti's Steakhouse.

Your Takeaways:

1. In both of these examples, offering to be a VITA site and to host the U.S. Census, were initially done because I felt they would benefit those we served. There was no money involved at the time of the initial collaborations. By doing things for the right reasons, money will come.

2. With a little effort and little or no money, with purposeful intent, the work you do can include and benefit other organizations, which in turn benefits the communities served.

3. Your website and your database can be a major marketing tool for local supporters.

Action Steps:

1. Make a list of the work, projects, and programs your organization are involved in.

2. Write down ways other organizations could compliment what you are doing, add value to those you are serving, that could benefit them, without costing your organization.

3. Make a list of what other organizations are doing that

you could compliment their operations, add value to those they serve, that could benefit you, without costing them anything.

4. Start contacting those organizations today.

5. Create a database or begin adding to it. See how you can benefit local businesses using your website and how those local businesses can benefit your organization in the long run.

Lesson #12

You Can't Be Too Big To Do The Little Things

The beginning for most executive directors is a passion for a cause or to right the ship of a worthy organization.

They want to help those in less fortunate situations or to help an organization that is doing the same.

The last thing an Executive Director thinks about doing (or wants to do) when first getting involved in the non-profit industry is raise money.

Fundraising is the number one reason Executive Directors finally burnout and leave the field. It's not the heartache, compassion and empathy that tugs at the heartstrings when working directly with a client. It's the never-ending game of raising money.

Executive Directors are always on the lookout for the one-big fundraiser.

I think this is mainly to have a brief break before starting to work on next year's big one.

Executive Directors and most boards alike don't want to work on 10-15 small fundraisers. They'd rather capitalize on one big event. Doesn't everyone? It's easy to understand why.

Unfortunately, this is a big mistake.

Time and again, I've seen board of directors and E.D.s, turn their noses up at funding streams because they appear to be too small.

I learned if you can generate funds, especially "unrestricted" funds, will little or no effort, regardless of the amount, you're foolish if you don't.

When it comes to raising money, as an Executive Director, I always look for innovative ways.

I believe if there is little or no effort required of my staff, volunteers, the board members, or myself, why not participate.

About six months ago, I received an email from Surveymonkey.com asking me to take a quick online survey. After taking the 2-3 minute survey, I was told fifty cents would be donated to a non-profit of my choice and I had a chance to win $100 gift card from Amazon.com.

I scrolled through the list and one of the biggest names was Boys Club of America. Many of the non-profits I'm familiar with, including those I consult with were not on the list.

I selected Boys Club of America. They received fifty cents for a few moments of my time.

After discovering this revenue stream that's available throughSurveymonkey.com, I contacted eight non-profits to inform them of this no-hassle, easy to implement fundraiser.

I suggested they ask their respective donor list, board members, staff, volunteers and all of their respective families and friends to participate. They could immediately begin to generate a revenue stream through Surveymonkey.com that would continue to grow over time.

I still receive requests to participate from Surveymonkey.com on a regular basis. If I don't have time or reply too late, it gives me a message there is no survey at this time.

I have now completed enough surveys over the past 6 plus months that Boys Club of America has received over $50.00 from my time, which has totaled less than an hour, when I was sitting in front of my computer anyway.

With 400 donors participating, that would generate $4,000 a year. With a 1,000 donors, you'd have $100,000.

The key is that it doesn't matter the amount of money. It's the type of money.

Someone takes 10-15 minutes to register the organization. You include instructions on how to register as a participant in your email signature block and you have a revenue stream that can grow.

I am still registered with Boys Club of American because none of the organizations thought it was worth taking the time to register.

I bet Boys Club of America think it was worth their time to register.

While leading one organization, Pepsi was running an online contest to award three non-profit organizations based on online voters.

I think at the time first prize was $15,000 and second and third were $10,000 each.

Each organization registered, stating what they did and what the money would be used for. I believe at the time the project had to serve youth.

There were state wide organizations, county organizations, and at least one drama organization that served youth internationally.

We were a small organization that served one community. Securing online voting to overtake organizations serving larger communities would be a big undertaking.

Through the commitment of staff and volunteers, I'm proud to say we took fifth. While we didn't receive an award, we were the highest ranking small non-profit.

Even in defeat, the staff and volunteers voting every day learned they could make a difference by participating.

There was daily excitement as we looked at the standings based on tallied votes. We kept thinking of other family and friends we could enlist to support our cause.

I do want to point out, prior to enrolling in any project or business that generates income for your non-profit, it is imperative that you check with your own financial advisors to ensure specific opportunities do not affect your non-profit status.

As I mentioned earlier in the book, programs such as Adopt-A-Poll through the County Registrar's Office are out there to help generate small amounts of money.

Another avenue for creating passive residual income for programs that serve youth is eScrip. Individuals sign up their Safeway cards and other cards. Each time a purchase is made at Safeway, Safeway donates a small percentage of the purchase to the organization you designation when you sign up. Some companies with their own credit card will commit to donating a certain percentage of each purchase you make to a designated non-profit organization.

I signed up to sponsor a friend's daughter when she was in high school. The cheerleading squad was using eScrip as a fundraiser.

My friend's daughter has graduated from college and is now a school teacher. My purchases at Safeway continue to sponsor the local high school's cheerleading squad as they have for more than ten years now.

Your Takeaways:

1. It's not the amount of money, but the type of money - passive residual income you can create from pockets of small opportunities that can grow larger over time with little or no effort from you.

2. People don't mind supporting organizations, especially when it doesn't cost them anymore of their net income.

3. Little streams lead to the rivers that lead to the ocean. Instead of thinking an opportunity is too small, focus on how you can use the small opportunity to increase your exposure in the community, build good will with other organizations and get others recognized. In the end, the money will come to you.

Action Steps:

1. Get volunteers to research direct marketing opportunities, affiliate marketing, etc. to see how many revenue streams you can create with little effort that can grow over time on their own.

2. Double check with your financial and legal advisors to ensure your organization remains in compliance with IRS requirements for a non-profit status.

3. Make sure your website encourages and asks visitors

to sign up on line for as many opportunities you have available through your organization and any links to affiliate programs are visible and easily accessible.

Lesson #13

Your Network Equals Your Net Worth

I don't know who originally make the comment "It's not what you know, but who you know that counts." In today's marketing world, with social media, these words have more meaning than ever before. It's the ones with the biggest network that will be successful.

Who you know, and even more importantly, who you know with influence, can be an incredible advantage for your organization.

There are two reasons for this. First, the way advertisers attracted new customers with the invention of radio and then television, are no longer effective.

Gone are the days when families sat around together and listened to radio shows.

There was a time when TV shows were watched from a box with rabbit ears. Since there were only three channels, as an advertiser, you had a good chance of getting the attention of 33% of the viewing audience.

Those days are long gone too.

While billboards are still found along highways in the Midwest and the South, advertising along highways has been reduced in California and some of the other highly populated states.

The reality is people are so busy looking at their phones, texting and reading texts, they don't have time to look at the road, let alone read billboard advertisements.

With the increasing methods for which to view programming, via the internet, cable companies, dish service providers, TV station websites, iphones, Smartphones, tablets and ipads, the consumers, the target market is no longer captive. With recording devices to fast-forward through commercials, and hoppers to skip commercials, statistics show advertising costs are rising and returns are diminishing.

Advertising is everywhere. There are video clips on the tops of gas station pumps. Logos are displayed on clothing. There are ads running along the side of websites on computers and banners run across the top or bottom of phone apps.

Consumers are bombarded with advertising, with estimates of each individual being exposed to over 2,000 ads per day. They no longer wait for a break in the TV program. They are coming at you! Pop up ads on the web, filling up at a gas station, wherever you are stuck - at intersections with heavy traffic, you can even find individuals flipping signs.

The more advertising we are bombarded with, the more we tune it out.

With each passing day, the greatest form of advertising, continues to increase in value.

The greatest form of advertising has been and always will be "word of mouth."

Recent surveys show only 14% of viewers will try what someone recommends in a TV ad, while 90% of those polled will try based on a recommendation from a friend.

Companies are realizing the best way to market products and services to acquire new customers is through individuals recommending their products and services to their families and friends.

In any business, there are two priorities. The first is to acquire customers. The second is to retain customers.

This brings us to the second reason why who you know and who you know with influence are so valuable for your organization.

When the U.S. actually manufactured products, company brands attracted "customer loyalty." If your grandfather drove a Ford, it was very likely your father drove a Ford, and you probably would've owned a Ford. Chevy owners passed their loyalty down from generation to generation as well.

This loyalty held with automobiles, brand of cigarettes, type of beer, all the way down to brands of clothing, i.e., Levis or Wranglers. Individuals and entire families would wear one brand, not both.

It didn't matter what the other brands costs or if the other options had more bells and whistles. Brand loyalty was passed down from generation to generation.

Now we have individuals with a pair of each brand of jeans; beer lovers rotate their brands of beer; commuters buy the car with the lowest price or the best gas mileage or some other factor besides the manufacturer.

With the ability to sell and purchase items over the internet, consumers have multiple options when it comes to every product. In addition to almost limitless brands, you can choose higher quality, average quality, multiple colors, different warranty limits, expensive and cheap, the variety is endless. You can buy local. You can buy around the world.

You can use a CPA firm down the street or hire one in another country. You may even hire the CPA firm down the street, who subcontracts the work to a firm in another country.

If you acquire a new customer for having the lowest price, you can count on losing that customer as soon as someone else has a lower price.

If you switch phone service or banks, you'll get cash offers to come back.

Customer retention has become a problem unto itself.

As with any problem, the customer retention problem also creates opportunities.

Opportunities your organization can capitalize on through its network.

Some businesses have learned to capitalize, some are in the process, and those that refused to learn are now out of business.

Those that have learned to capitalize on these opportunities, have discovered the secrets to customer retention through the use of networks.

Here are the two secrets...

1. Most people, including me, will do more for others than we will do for ourselves.

   For example, you get home late, you've settled down to watch TV and you realize you forgot to buy milk. Rather than get up and go to the store, you decide to go early in the morning. Moments later, a friend calls saying he is at the store and his car won't start. You tell him you'll be right there with jumper cables.

2. Everybody likes to buy, but nobody likes to be sold.

For example, you go into a store to buy a shirt. A salesperson comes along and asks if you need help. The majority of responses are the same. "No thank you. I'm just looking."

Knowing that as human beings, most of us like to help others and we like to buy, but don't want to be sold anything, businesses are able to use this information to retain customers.

Let's use banks for example. As I mentioned earlier, if you switch banks, it's very likely, your former bank will contact you and say, "We want your business back. Come back to us, and with your first direct deposit, we'll give you a $100, deposited right into your account." This type of attempt to get back lost customers happens frequently.

While leading a non-profit organization, a representative from a fast growing bank, BBVA Compass, approached me about moving our accounts to their bank.

They were offering an "easy, hassle-free fundraising program" for non-profit organizations, just like ours.

At the time of this writing, their program, "Compass for Your Cause" is still available in certain states, California being one. (Please check with BBVA in your area for specific details, qualifications and other requirements.)

The following is for example purposes only and does not create liability for the bank.

Compass for Your Cause Program offers a $50 donation for each bank account the non-profit opens at their bank. Additionally, with each qualifying purchase made using a bank debit card, 0.25% of those qualifying purchases will be donated back to the non-profit.

With each supporter of the non-profit coming into the bank and opening up accounts, the non-profit will receive a $50 donation per account opened. With each supporter that uses a bank debit card on qualifying purchases, the non-profit will also receive 0.25% of their qualifying purchases.

BBVA Compass even offers to put the non-profit logo on the debit cards to remind your supporters, their customers, that they are supporting your organization with each qualifying purchase.

This program uses both secrets to cover the two top priorities of any business.

The first priority is acquiring customers. It's not thrilling to change banks. It's not hard, but can be an inconvenience, making sure outstanding checks have cleared before closing the account, etc.

Unless you feel you've been gouged by your bank, most people will remain where they are at indefinitely.

However, (Secret #1, We do more for others than we do for ourselves), when you ask donors, employees, family, friends, etc., to do you a favor, help your organization, and those you serve, by changing banks, most will do you a favor and switch.

When you explain your organization will benefit long-term by receiving a quarter percentage of their purchases made with their debit card, purchases they would make anyway, what friend, what supporter would turn down a request to help a worthy organization like yours?

Here's where the secrets cover the second priority, customer retention.

Those that have switched to help your organization, will start to receive calls from their former bank, asking them to come back. Most will be offered some monetary sum to do so.

However, (Secret #2, We like to buy but don't want to be sold) because they know you and/or your organization, they know they have done you a favor. They know they are doing some good. The majority will respond, "Thank you. I appreciate the offer. However, I'm helping out a friend and his/her organization. So, I'm staying put no matter what the offer."

These kind of marketing strategies (referred to as relationship marketing) tailored to use networks are becoming more and more of the norm.

It's the way direct sales and network marketing began and thrive today.

Recently, Sprint Wireless has been advertising "Framily Plans" giving groups of friends and family discounts by offering bigger discounts the more people that join your "Framily."

They are focusing on acquiring new customers by helping their existing customers to bring on family and friends, thereby saving all of them some monthly costs on their respective phones.

The feeling among the "Framily" is they are a part of

something bigger than themselves. They are benefitting by the group participation. If they leave the group, the discount will reduce hurting those remaining in the "Framily." Talk about customer retention!

It's the same concept when a restaurant or store offers a gift card for referring a friend.

Your Takeaways:

1. Your network of family, friends, and business associates are valuable to other businesses.

2. If you have the influence, the ability to ask those in your network to help your organization by supporting another business, buying in bulk, etc., the value goes way up.

3. You can leverage the value of your network for immediate, short-term and long-term benefits.

Action Steps:

1. Talk to the nearest BBVA Bank in your area. Check with your current bank or other local banks to see if they have a program for non-profits.

2. Look over your contacts within your organization, ask board members and staff members to look over their personal contacts. See what businesses and industries could benefit from the purchasing power of those networks.

3. Set up meetings with those businesses to determine the benefits they could contribute to your organization if the networks purchased their products and/or services.

Lesson #14

If You're Not Helping Row The Boat, You're An Anchor

During my career, I've sat on multiple boards (and continue to serve on two currently). I've helped develop boards, trained boards, and written board member manuals. I've also had the experience of working for and with eclectic boards while serving as Executive Director for different organizations.

The stories I could share could fill a series of books. Many would cause you to laugh hysterically, while others would make you cry. I say this because that's what I experienced through each of them, as well as most of the emotions in between.

Through every experience, good, bad, happy or sad, I am grateful for being a part of each one. I acquired incredible knowledge from so many of the board members I served under. Every experience has played a role in helping me become the person I am today.

I'm able to shorten the learning curve for new Executive Directors. I'm able to coach and support executive directors and boards going through difficult times based on what I learned from being in the trenches.

With that said, I contemplated whether to include a chapter on board of directors. With a purpose of helping executive directors, board of directors, and organizations, I felt I needed to make a few comments, if for no other reason than to give executive directors some ammunition when trying to engage their respective boards.

Regardless of what other books will tell you regarding the roles, responsibilities, and duties of board of directors, the bottom line is, regardless of what type of non-profit the organization is, board members need to bring funds into an organization. The only exception may be a board member that is saving their non-profit money. For example, an attorney on the board of directors that handles legal matters pro bono or at a significantly reduced rate.

When I'm asked to serve on a board of directors, I expect to make a contribution, so I ask right up front, "What is the contribution level expected of board members?"

Obviously, time commitments are also a big factor in making a commitment.

Earlier, I mentioned while speaking before a City Council, I pointed out that Requests for Proposals from U.S. Federal Grants, as well as many others, ask "Who are your other funders?" They do this to see if there is local support, and use the list of funders as a "rubber stamp" of approval regarding the quality of services provided.

Another question most Requests for Proposals ask is "What is the level of board contribution?" They do not ask for the dollar amounts contributed by the board. They do want to know if 100% of the board contributes or if only 65% or none of the board contributes.

In instances, where two organizations have submitted proposals and the scoring is tight or tied, the percentage of board contribution can make the difference.

Some foundations will reject proposals if a certain level of board contribution is not met. A lack of board support can be a deal breaker.

I have shared my stories on how I challenged my boards with Payroll Contribution Programs, asking them to match employee contributions, with good success.

The following example didn't reach the level of success I had hoped for.

One of my first experiences working with a board of directors was different than most executive directors experience. My board had never contributed to the organization. In fact, the non-profit had no previous fundraising activities.

This particular board met monthly and at each meeting, those attending received a free lunch.

Over my first 8-10 months, the board was pleased with my vision, the plan, its implementation and the progress to date.

I had implanted the Employee Payroll Contribution Plan and had put out my initial challenge to the board. I announced the challenge at a monthly meeting and asked them to respond by the next month's meeting.

As the next meeting was fast approaching, not one of the board members had contacted me regarding making a contribution.

At the meeting, I laid out a fund development plan explaining I would commit to raising $1,500 or donating $1,500. I included in the plan for each board member to raise $500 or to make a contribution in that amount or the difference between what was raised and the $500 goal.

My plan included ways they could help with fundraising. The simplest suggestion was to have a coffee cake party at their respective homes.

I laid out a game plan, including an invite script for the members to use. It went something like this:

Each board member would call their friends and/or business associates and invite them over for coffee and cake. On the call, the board member would say, "Hi, Joe. Do you have a minute? You know I serve on the board of directors for XYZ, a non-profit doing great things for disadvantaged individuals and families living in our community. I'm proud of the work they do and the benefits our residents receive. On Saturday, I'm having a little get-together at my place for about an hour. I'm inviting you and nine others to come and learn a little about what we do. The Executive Director will be here to answer questions and he's bringing an individual to tell you his story of how XYZ has impacted his life. Between the 10 of you, I'm hoping to raise $500. Can I count on you to do me a favor, and show up with your checkbook? It would really mean a lot to me and the organization."

If they couldn't make it, I suggested asking for a $25 check, or whatever they could afford. The worst case scenario is the friend would say, "I'm sorry, but not right now."

A few of the board members stated they would raise the $500 through their own efforts. One board member missed the meeting and never returned. When it came to the last board member, she just broke down in tears. It startled me as I had never seen a board member cry.

She partially composed herself and through her tears said she didn't have any friends that could afford $50, and she wouldn't ask any of her friends to make a contribution to the organization. She reached in her purse and pulled out a five dollar bill. She said, "Here, take this. It's all I can afford to contribute.

She wasn't interested in participating in any type of fundraising.

I did my best to calm her down. I said no one was being forced to contribute financially. I told her I would sit down with her the following week to see if we could put our heads together and come up with another way for her to participate.

With the reluctance of some members to contribute, I had to look at other ways to offset the lack of funds being generated.

It was decided that feeding the board at each meeting would stop. They were welcome to bring a bag lunch. At $7-$8 per member for a deli sandwich and drink, we saved about $100 per month, $1,200 a year.

After meeting with the emotional board member, she acknowledged she wasn't contributing anything to the meetings except her personal opinion on agenda topics, which other individuals in a board member position could do, plus additional tasks, like raising money.

She graciously stepped down from the board of directors. She did agree to stay on as a volunteer as a part-time receptionist/greeter and advocate for our clients.

Your TAKEAWAYS:

1. An organization is like a boat bouncing around on the waves. It takes everyone in the boat to row their oar to get the boat to where we want it to go.

2. If you're not participating, helping row the boat, you become dead weight. You're filling a spot that could be used by someone else that would gladly participate.

3. If you can't contribute financially, at least help save on expenses. Either way, you are enhancing the organization you believe in.

4. As an Executive Director, plans drawn up on paper, ideas shared in meetings, more often than not, will produce something unexpected. You may experience someone leaving and not coming back. You may have someone breakdown emotionally. Regardless of the unexpected, you cannot let the bumps along the way, stop you from taking action to move you closer to your goals.

5. The key is to keep coming up with ideas and plans; along with alternatives when they don't go as expected.

ACTION STEPS:

1. Do an assessment of each board member; include their strengths and weaknesses, evaluate their influence over other board members. Make sure you know "why" each board member is volunteering their time with your organization. What gives value to each one. Doing this will allow you to make requests of each member knowing ahead of time, the value they will receive in handling the tasks.

2. Make sure you have the influencers up to speed on agenda items before board meetings.

3. Make a point to sit down individually with each of your board members in advance of a meeting. Get their input on establishing a "give or get" amount for board members to acquire each year.

4. If you don't have a fundraising plan manual for your board members, draft one up, listing fundraising ideas that can be discussed and implemented over time.

5. Be sure to include in your fundraising ideas a "quarterly event" that can be implemented over time. For example, if you already have an annual summer event, get a committee to oversee implementing an annual winter event. The following year add another volunteer committee to oversee a new annual fall event. The next year, you can add a fourth committee, focusing only on their respective annual event, this one being an annual spring event.

6. Each event should be totally different and could have a different target market for supporters. For example, maybe you host a spring-cleaning event, utilizing a large parking lot for residents to rent a parking space and hold a community yard sale. In the summer, you can sponsor a spaghetti feed; in the fall, you can sponsor an end of summer dance for students; and in the winter hold a Holiday Ballroom Dance.

Lesson #15

Do You Know What An Outhouse Is

Whether you are an experienced Executive Director, just beginning, or desire to be one in the future, I hope throughout this book, you have been able to feel my exhilaration when following my core beliefs, my beliefs resonated true. For example, I believe that if you do the right things for the right reasons, the money will come to you.

Multiple times throughout this book, I've provided real examples of this belief becoming realities.

I also hope that through the details in some of my experiences, you can sense the frustration that comes after putting yourself out there, being ridiculed by board members, and having to overcome opposition from those within your own organization.

I know from personal experience there are two clues that will confirm you are a leader. The first clue is if you feel like someone or a group of people are kicking you in your behind. The second clue is when it feels like someone or a group of people are stabbing you in the back.

In both cases, getting kicked in the behind and/or getting stabbed in the back, requires you being out front.

Once, when I went to interview for an Executive Director position, the hiring committee told me their organization had a strong foundation. They were looking for someone to take them to the next level.

After assuring them I was the right person to take the organization to the next level, they asked me for ideas I would have for fundraising.

I started off with my philosophy of providing value first, then asking for contributions.

I concluded with an idea I thought to be innovative and a new approach for raising funds as a non-profit.

I explained I had recently been introduced to a network marketing business opportunity. I pointed out network marketing businesses are tailored for individuals and success comes from a system that can be duplicated, meaning individuals finding more individuals willing to work within the company's system.

As a thought leader, I said the program would work with non-profits. I explained how I saw each non-profit organization as an individual within the network marketing company's system.

This particular network marketing company sold home services that people use every day. Services that people are already paying for. The difference would be to have the people re-route their expenditures through the non-profit and then the network marketing company would receive a percentage of the bills paid and then a percentage would go to the individuals (or organizations signing up the customers).

Two things make this concept an incredible opportunity. First, when funds are low, making donations is one of the first thing families cut back on. With this plan, people are already spending money on these services. Basically, by signing up, you're allowing the service providers to refund a percentage of your bill to the non-profit.

Let's use garbage collection as an example. Let's say you pay $50 a month. Through this network marketing company, you can get trash collected for the same price, through another company, however, the network marketing company will pay you 10% of the bill. So for a $50 trash collection bill each month, you'll receive $5.

When you are asking individuals for donations, they say they are short on cash. You ask if they pay for garbage collection. They say yes. You ask them if they would be willing to donate $5 a month, if it didn't cost them any money. With a puzzled look they say yes.

You ask them to switch over their garbage collection to another company for the same price.

You're probably thinking $5 a month isn't much. However, that's just one service in one house. There may be 4-5 more services in that one house. At $5 for each service, you're now looking at $20-$25 per month from one household.

If you work in a school district, you know there are boundaries. For this particular non-profit, they had over 10,000 households in their surrounding areas.

At $20-$25 per household, you're looking at $200-$250K a month.

What's really exciting about this part is many times (depending on the networking company) the products and services are offered by national or international companies. This means the potential donors expands from the 10,000 homes in the school district and now includes grandparents, friends and other relatives that live out of state and possibly in other countries.

Allow yourself to let this concept soak in. Your organization can have the potential of an unlimited funding stream of unrestricted funds.*

The second part of this concept is you can get paid off of other people's customers as well. This means by helping other non-profits do exactly what you've done, you'll get paid on their customers too.

For example, you get paid 10% of your customers' bills. For each organization you enroll in the program (acts as one of your customers), your organization will receive 10% of the organization' direct bills. This equates to $5 for every $50 eligible service bill. As organization LMP signs up their own customers, they'll receive 10% of their respective customers' bills. In addition, you'll receive a smaller percentage of LMP's customer bills as well, even though you didn't do any work to acquire LMP's customers. For example, let's say you receive 2% of your LMP's customers' bills. In this scenario, while LMP will get $5 for one of their customer's $50 service bill, you will earn an additional 2% of that same $50 service bill (equal to one dollar).

You actually help other struggling organizations (in this case LMP) remain viable with a new cash flow opportunity, but you also earn 2% of every customer's bill that LMP earns 5% on.

This is monthly revenues that will continue to grow, as customers (supporters sign up their services) and they pay month after month.

The question always arises, how can these home service companies pay out 5% and 2%? More and more companies are shifting their advertising dollars to relationship marketing companies.

Instead of paying $3M for a 30-second Super Bowl

commercial, they offer a network marketing company that $3M to get their representatives to talk to people about their products and services.

When a customer is acquired - and only when a customer is acquired, does the service company pay out the 5% and 2% for customer acquisition. They will pay it every month afterwards for customer retention.

We all talk, talk, and talk to friends and family about things we like, purchases we've made, etc. We just don't get paid if others follow our recommendations and acquire what we did.

Companies will love paying only for acquired customers over paying advertising up front and hoping to get customers in return. It's a no-brainer.

The hiring committee must've liked the idea because I got the job.

After a few months on the job, going through a personal orientation, learning more about the organization, I decided it was time to implement the fundraising program.

Prior to presenting it at the board meeting, I went to meet with each individual board member (that wasn't on the hiring committee) to share my idea with them and to ask for their support.

I had a similar experience with two of my board members. Both were executives employed by two different governmental agencies.

With each one, after explaining my idea, I asked them what they thought and if they would support me in voting to approve the fundraising program.

One started laughing and said he thought it was a stupid idea. The other appeared agitated and stated he thought I was an idiot.

While frustrated internally, I smiled at each one and asked, "Do you know what an outhouse is?"

Independently, each one said of course and asked what that had to do with my fundraising plan.

I said imagine an outhouse on a hot summer day, with the smell and the flies. You hear a knock at the door and when you open it, a man tells you he would like to move your outhouse inside, next to the kitchen, and use running water to flush it after every use.

I bet you would have laughed in his face and said he was an idiot.

However, he just went next door, and kept going door-to-door until someone said, do it.

Once it was in the house and flushed with running water, the owner had everyone in town come by and see it work. Then everybody that laughed wanted one.

Now the guy who invented the indoor toilet is sitting somewhere on a mountain top laughing at the world.

I told both of them, eye to eye, "You can think the idea is stupid or that I am an idiot. The bottom line is my paycheck comes from being able to raise funds, yours doesn't. If it doesn't work, you can tell everyone that you told me so. If it does work, I'll say I couldn't have done it without your support. While I cannot guarantee that it will work, I think it will. I can guarantee you this. If it doesn't work, I will try something else. If that doesn't work, I will continue trying something else until I find something that does or you get tired of watching my attempts and fire me."

Both shook their head and said okay.

Unfortunately, the story doesn't stop there. The program was initially approved. However, one of the two governmental executives couldn't stand the idea. He put so much pressure on the supporters of the program, the board was splitting into sides, so I said we would just withdraw from the program.

The animosity created from the different perspectives resulted in the board asking me to get some coaching. I agreed as long as the coaching wasn't from any of the existing board members.

I explained I was hired to take the organization to the next level. I needed to be coached by someone that had taken an organization to the next level. With all due respect, their coaching wouldn't afford me that opportunity, as they had no experience taking an organization to the next level.

I let the board select a coach. I am always open to learning from someone that has more experience, more education, and more wisdom. While the board thought it was punitive, I was actually excited.

When a coach was selected and we finally met, I shared the fund raising fiasco with him. He said, "Bryan, it's a great idea. It's just ahead of its time."

He went on to share a story when he was the Executive Director of a National Non-Profit. He had heard of this fund raising idea, which at the time was only being done by the Polly Klaus Foundation in Marin County.

They had started a "donate-a-car" program, whether it was

running or not. The program was generating one million dollars a month in donations.

My coach said when he presented it to his board, they looked at him and said, "We're not in the car business. Our mission statement doesn't have anything to do with the automotive industry."

He said, now, 10 years later, almost all national non-profits, including the one he tried to implement the program with, were accepting donated cars, trucks, boats and motorcycles. He said there are even non-profits that do nothing but collect donated cars and give them to other non-profits.

Your TAKEAWAYS:

1. When you are leading, you're not on the beaten path. You are blazing new trails. People are afraid of the unknown, afraid of making mistakes. You will face opposition to almost every idea, sometimes the opposition is stronger than at other times, but there will be opposition nonetheless.

2. You should always try to gain consensus one-on-one initially as those opposed to your ideas will do everything possible to influence your supporters to support the opposition's point of view.

3. Even when you are accountable and take responsibility for the outcomes, get consensus ahead of time, and have communicated your vision from day one, sometimes things just don't work out.

4. While it's frustrating at times that others cannot see your vision and can be extremely difficult not to take it personally, you have to realize it comes down to

timing.

5. In order to get to the next level, to go where you haven't been before, you have to do things you've never done before. You have to learn from people that have done what you want to do.

ACTION STEPS:

1. Start a Mastermind Group. Ask a few successful people, in different industries to meet once a month to kick around ideas, a brainstorming session, where everyone benefits from getting perspectives from leaders in other areas.

2. Look over past ideas that were discarded for one reason or another. It could have been a timing issue then. It may be the right time now.

3. Get some volunteers to help search online for fundraising events other organizations are doing. The organizations do not have to be in your area, preferably they are across the country or in other countries. See if their events would work for your organization; or see if you can get ideas from their events that would work for you.

4. Never give up. With each idea, with each attempt, you are experiencing growth. You are learning valuable information. Evaluate each rejection. Have someone critique the experience for you. You may need to improve the presentation, maybe provide more supporting data, or find more people to support your ideas. Whatever the reason, you won't know for sure until you evaluate the results and then work on improving. You can do it!

Lesson #16

Sometimes Two Organizations Are Better Than One

I can't remember who said it first, but there is a lot of truth to the statement, "some of my best ideas were someone else's ideas."

I don't think duplicating the same fundraisers other organizations in your area are doing is the smartest thing to do.

After all, how many "all-you-can-eat crab feeds" do you think a donor wants to attend in a year? It doesn't take long until each organization is trying to have their crab feed first.

What I do think is a great concept is one of combining two events, where a donor can benefit two organizations at the same time.

I attempted to utilize this approach while serving in my last role as an Executive Director. Unfortunately, scheduling conflicts prevented the two-fold approach from materializing.

I have participated in several as a supporter and individual donor.

My experiences, both times, centered around a "Pancake Breakfast" which were being held by local civic organizations. The first was a Rotary Club and the other event was hosted by a Lions Club.

In addition to raising funds for their local clubs, they partnered with the American Red Cross for a blood drive.

The American Red Cross set up trailers with tables for

donors.

After making a contribution and eating breakfast, donors would voluntarily give blood, benefitting two different organizations in one morning.

Often times, events of this nature will bring out blood donors that may or may not attend civic group fundraisers and vice versa.

However, with both organizations present at the same time, each may receive more donations than normal, because some blood donors will donate and eat a breakfast, just as some civic group supporters will also decide to donate blood.

This is a great example where two organizations can benefit one another by holding an event together.

I would not recommend holding an event where both organizations are seeking monetary contributions. In this event, it could actually be detrimental. A donor may try to accommodate both by splitting his/her donation to benefit both organizations, thereby reducing the individual donation one organization may have received on its own.

Regardless of the roles of the two participating organizations, this approach can be initiated by either one.

Your TAKEAWAYS:

1. By strategizing with other organizations, you can increase the likelihood of improving the turnout for a fundraising event.

2. With the attendance of supporters for two different organizations, you increase the likelihood of both organizations receiving the benefit of crossover

support from the other organization's donors.

3. At the very least, both organizations benefit from being able to educate potential donors from those attending in support of the other organization.

Action Steps:

1. Make a list of organizations that you could assist by inviting them to participate in one of your fundraisers. The list could include blood donors, libraries for book drives, environmental groups to help clean a local lake or park, etc.

2. Contact these organizations and see if they have upcoming events that your organization and donor list could participate in to help their cause.

3. Take the time to schedule coffee or lunch with the leaders of local organizations and see if there are opportunities where you could collaborate for an event. You may find creative ideas that would allow for multiple groups to participate in a community event that would benefit the residents and all of the groups participating.

4. See if there is a way you can benefit local residents with one of your upcoming events. For example give local start-up bands some exposure by allowing them to play at your event or a combined event.

About The Author

Bryan Balch, a certified life coach, is an advocate of personal development. He considers himself a lifetime student, always striving for constant and never-ending improvement. For over a decade, Bryan has shared and taught personal development to individuals, groups and organizations.

Bryan's career focus has been to improve the lives of others.

He has led multiple organizations, developing strategies and implementing programs serving disadvantaged populations including individuals with disabilities; seniors and the elderly; low-income residents, immigrants; the under-employed and unemployed; and troubled youth, young adults, offenders and ex-offender populations.

Bryan engages with entire communities including school districts, business owners, community-based organizations, residents, and governmental entities at all levels.

Bryan is committed to his work as a life coach, working with those seeking change. He works with individuals and businesses through his coaching, consulting, speaking and writing.

In addition to the non-profit world, Bryan's entrepreneurial spirit has provided him with experience owning a maintenance business, a sporting goods business, a real estate acquisition partnership, and has executive experience in the storage facilities industry. His diverse work experience also includes telecommunications and network marketing.

Described as a thought leader, social entrepreneur, business owner, author, father, grandfather, son, brother and friend to many, Bryan desires to leave a legacy of significance. Most people wish for success. Many even achieve success. Bryan explains that achieving success is not enough. He believes everything we can achieve we have a responsibility to teach others how to achieve it. Significance is being able to help others become successful.

Bryan is passionate about his work, a true believer that there is greatness within everyone and that all services are needed to make a community whole.

When he's not writing, reading or assisting others, Bryan focuses his energies in other areas, working to create a balance in all areas of life for true wealth.

Bryan enjoys spending time with his family and strengthening his spirituality.

Bryan is an avid sports fan. When he's not playing baseball or softball, he enjoys watching competitive sports at all levels. Bryan is also striving to increase his time at the gym, believing that without your health, nothing else will matter.

Bryan lives a life of gratitude. He is thankful for the opportunity to connect with more people through his writings.

Bryan appreciates you taking the time to read his book and prays that you receive value for the time you invested in reading this book as well as any monetary investment.

Bryan applauds you for being a member of the minority; the small percentage of people that are making the effort to become more than they are; willing to expand your mind, hear different perspectives; striving to overcome fear of failure to take more risks; continually seeking improvement; living a life with purpose; serving others.

Bryan invites you to stay connected and extends the invitation to those you think would benefit from being connected.

As this book goes to distribution, Bryan is already working on two new books. You can subscribe to his weekly Monday Morning Thoughts on his website. You can follow him on Twitter and post your comments on his Facebook page. You can also connect with him via LinkedIn, where he is now publishing weekly posts.

If you learn something of value from this book, maybe a new idea that makes a difference in your life let Bryan know. Your success stories and comments mean the world to him.

To Connect With Bryan

Website: http://bryanbalch.com
Twitter: http://twitter.com/bryanbalch
Facebook: http://facebook.com/bryan.m.balch
LinkedIn: http://linkedin.com/in/bryanbalch
E-mail: bb@bryanbalch.com

Consultations And Presentations

Bryan Balch is available for individual and organizational consultations. Bryan is an experienced presenter and trainer for staff, volunteers and board of directors. Each training and presentation can be tailored to meet your specific needs.

For cost and availability, contact Bryan through any of the links above.

All of the services offered by Bryan Balch come with a money back guarantee.

Other Publications

If you enjoyed this book, you may also enjoy his book:

Understanding What Needs to be Understood, Dec. 2012

Available in multiple formats at:

www.smashwords.com
www.amazon.com
www.barnesandnoble.com
and other major ebook retailers

Added Bonus(es)

By now, you know Bryan Balch walks the talk in his belief in creating value first.

Bryan also believes that the best way to create and maintain long-term success, and long-term relationships is to always over-deliver.

For having purchased this book, either as an ebook, or in printed format (paperback), regardless of your purchase price, Bryan values his relationship with you.

1. With the copy of a receipt for your purchase, Bryan will provide a free 30-minute consultation with you, by phone on any topic that will benefit you and/or your organization.

   This $75 value is provided by Bryan as a thank you for your purchase and to develop a two-way relationship with his readers.

2. With the copy of a receipt for a single purchase of 10 copies, Bryan will provide a one-hour consultation by phone, in person, or video conference for up to 10 people, valued at $250. Bryan is committed to helping you get to where you want to go, providing you an abundance of value along the way.

Third Bonus

3. With a single receipt indicating the purchase of 15 books, a 90 minute presentation, valued at $400 will be made by Bryan Balch for a group up to 30 people at no cost. Method of presentation will be determined by geographic limitations.

All three bonus offers expire on January 31, 2015 and are subject to availability. For more info connect with Bryan.

NOTES

NOTES

www.ingramcontent.com/pod-product-compliance
Lightning Source LLC
Chambersburg PA
CBHW051731170526
45167CB00002B/892